Revenue Management 101: Using Effective Techniques to Increase Revenues and Asset Value

Bob Copper
Self Storage 101
866-269-1311

Copyright 2012 Birmingham, AL

FORWARD

If you are the onsite manager of a self-storage facility you have a great deal of responsibility for the success of your facility. Unlike working in a large retail store or factory where there are large numbers of employees, it is highly likely that you are oftentimes the only person on duty at your site. Your ability to rent space, collect money and get it all done using effective time management are going to be the factors that determine whether or not your facility meets its expectations.

'Learning from the successful' is the first and most important step in your transition from a property care-taker to a self-storage professional. Your willingness to learn new skills, practice new techniques and utilize new ideas will increase both your value to the company you work for and the market competitiveness of the facility you manage.

Keep working to increase your ability to rent space even when it is a challenge. Keep working to increase your effectiveness in collecting rent even when you would rather be doing something else. And keep working on perfecting your time management skills so you can get it all done, get it all done well and have a rich and rewarding life outside of storage.

Bob Copper
Partner in Charge
Self Storage 101

Revenue Management 101: Using Effective Techniques to Increase Revenues and Asset Value

CAUTION: DO NOT read this book if you DO NOT want or need to make more money! But, if you do want or need to make more money, read on!

Why should you go through the 'trouble' if implementing strategies or policies or procedures that are intended to help you make more money?

- **Are your expenses increasing?** If your expenses are continuing to increase but you are not actively working to increase your revenue you are going backward.
- **Do you want to see an increase in value?** Why shouldn't your self-storage investment be like all of your other investments? You bought or built it to increase the value, right?
- **Considering a refinance?** It may be time to take advantage of historically low interest rates, perhaps take some equity out of your facility but in order to do that you really need to implement revenue-increase procedures.
- **What about your legacy?** If you plan to hand your facility or portfolio down to future generations, just exactly what will they inherit? Have you put systems in place to maximize the value?
- **Thinking about selling?** If a potential buyer comes calling you cannot ask them to come back in a year to give you time to 'clean up' your operation and increase revenues. Those 'systems' should be in place at all times.

Why does it really matter?

Because it's all about increasing the NOI: 'net operating income'. Every dollar-per-month increase in revenues can equal an approximate $150 in additional value added to your self storage asset. EVERY dollar really does matter.

Our experience indicates that far too many owner/operators are leaving too much money 'on the table' because they do not have effective revenue management systems in place. Whether to refinance or sell, understanding how to increase the net operating income will have a profound impact on how much value you realize for your storage assets.

We have found that there are three primary reasons owner/operators fail to maximize the value of their assets and so therefore leave 'free money' on the table:

- **Lack of Knowledge.** Frankly, many otherwise well-meaning operators just don't know what to do as it relates to increasing revenues and asset value. They are hanging on 'by the seat of their pants' as it is so effectively implementing revenue management systems is more than likely not going to happen.

  - The reality is the wealth of resources available in the self storage business is overwhelming.
  - Learn to take advantage of those resources!
  - The quicker you realize that 'how you used to do it' is not working anymore the quicker you can implement proven strategies for improving revenues and value.
  - Understand that it's okay to not know everything but it is not okay to fail to do something about it.

- **Ego.** Since many self storage operators are 'self made' men and women they sometimes struggle with admitting that they really don't know everything.

  - Remember that you really don't have to the smartest guy (or lady) in the room.
  - History shows that the most successful people surround themselves with smart people.
  - We find that people with large egos tend to get left behind by those with smart teams.

- **Lack of Planning.** You may never plan to sell your facility but you should always manage the operation as if you would today if someone offered you enough money. Don't lose out on additional asset value and money because you failed to plan effectively.

  - Learn to make your pursuit of knowledge applicable to your operation. If you attend a seminar or buy a book or pay a high-priced consultant for their information but fail to implement any of the good ideas, what was the point?
  - Don't just focus on today. Increasing revenues and asset value is an exercise that unfolds over the long term.
  - Doing something now, no matter how small or seemingly insignificant, could have far reaching effects. Implementing a modest existing tenant increase today or keeping a closer eye on the climate controlled thermostats might seem petty right now but could have real impact on the value down the road.

Steps for Increasing Revenues

There are a number of steps an owner/operator needs to consider when undertaking the serious project of increasing revenues, and ultimately the value, of their self storage assets:

- **Rent more space**
- **Reduce discounts**
- **Increase Street Rates**
- **Increase Rents to Existing Tenants**
- **Increase Ancillary Income**
- **Improve collections**

ANOTHER CAUTION: It's ALWAYS About the Manager!

Regarding a Manager Review

This revenue/value improvement exercise MIGHT require a manager change. Do you have a 'babysitter' or a professional salesperson managing your multi-million dollar investment? Your manager might not be able to do what needs to be done.

Before implementing a substantial amount of the processes, systems and techniques in this manual we HIGHLY recommend that onsite management be at the very least afforded the opportunity to be exposed to training in effective sales and collections skills.

Step One: Rent More Space

No other step, process, seminar, book or expensive lecture will make a difference at your site unless you figure out this self storage secret: ***There's no way around it: You HAVE to Rent More Units!***

The first step all self storage owner/operators must address is learning to Increase Revenues by Increasing Occupancy. Clearly 'rental income' makes up the largest and most important percentage of facility revenue and a laser focus on the manager's most important task –renting space – will have the most immediate and powerful impact on a facility's revenues.

- **Implement Professional Sales Skills Training.** The days of 'build it and they will come' are long since over and how skilled a self storage manager is in using an effective sales presentation really does matter now. No longer can an owner/operator afford to tolerate or 'get by' with a manager who has no sales skills.
- **Develop and Implement Effective Marketing.** When's the last time you took the time to track your marketing efforts? Do you really know what does and does not work? What does and what does not offer an acceptable return on investment? Learn what marketing efforts generate traffic and phone calls and quit using those that help with neither.
- **Learn How to Use Premiums Instead of Deep Discounts to Rent More Space.** It's probably a bit naïve to believe you can successfully compete in the current self storage climate without offering some kind of move-in promotion. Unfortunately the lack of investment in effective sales skills has resulted in offering far too much in free rent as the most preferred move-in incentive. This can have a devastating impact on your efforts to increase revenues and value.

We recommend the use, when necessary, of 'premiums' to close a rental instead of giving away free rent.

- Premiums can have a higher perceived value than discounted rent.
    - FREE move in pak
        - Made up of a few boxes, tape and bubble wrap
        - Actual cost of those items is far less than the perceived value.
    - FREE lock
    - FREE rental truck
- Remember that lost rent is lost forever!

Notes regarding increasing occupancy:

It is important to Create a Sense of Urgency at your facility regarding renting space. A 'ho-hum' attitude about the most important task managers should undertake will be highly detrimental to the success of your facility.

Keep in mind:

- Vacant space has very little value. Do you know the value of a rental at your facility? If not, why not? You will more clearly understand the sense of urgency when you know how much each rental is really worth.
- You cannot increase rates on vacant space. An important step in increasing revenues and value is to implement existing tenant increases. You can't do that on vacant space.
- It is very expensive to NOT rent space. Consider:
    - The cost of generating leads can be significant and wasteful if professional effort is not put into maximizing those leads and turning a higher percentage of leads into rentals.
    - A unit not rented equals lost rental income and lost value increase.

- A unit not rented means lost ancillary sales potential. You likely not going to sell boxes, rent a truck or collect insurance premiums from a non-tenant.

You will also increase your chances of renting to a higher percentage of your potential self storage leads if you make sure your facility is 'rent ready' at all times.

- Insure site has great curb appeal. Take another good look at your facility and 'see that the customer sees'. Is the look appealing and inviting or dirty and unprofessional?

- Make sure all your vacant units are clean and 'ready-to rent'. Your prospective tenants will lose confidence in your professional abilities if you show them storage units that are dirty, containing trash or damaged and otherwise unrentable. If you have a large number of vacant spaces at least make sure you have a number of each unit size clean and rent ready and that you know which of those units to show prospective customers.

'Increasing occupancy' is a two-pronged approach:

- Maximizing efforts to turn more prospects into tenants, and
- Implementing policies and procedures to encourage tenants to stay. You can do that by:

  o Learning how to provide a superior customer service experience for your tenants. Although most self storage customers vacate their space because they no longer need the space there are a number that vacate due to poor customer service.

- Keep your promises.
- Keep the facility and restrooms clean.
- Maintain the security features of your facility.
- Establish positive rapport with your customers.
  - Use effective collections techniques to reduce auction sales. Although it is nearly impossible to completely eliminate lien auctions, it is clearly proven that the number of auctions can be reduced by using professional collections skills.
    - Get good information at the time of the rental.
    - Implement a collections system.
    - Follow up on broken commitments to make payment.

Why is it critical to give renting units the sense of urgency that is deserves?

"Because every rental counts!"

What is just one extra rental per week over a year's time worth to your site?

Assume you are able to start next year with 52 more units occupied than you did last year:

- 52 more units on rent
- average of $100/month rental rate
- average stay of 10 months
- $1000 average value
- Extra $52,000 per year in rental income!

An extra $52,000 per year in rental income JUST BY RENTING ONE EXTRA UNIT PER WEEK!

And how can you end this year with 52 more rentals than last year?

- Sell one less unit at auction per month – 12 additional units on rent
- Gain one more referral per month – 12 additional units on rent
- Have one less dissatisfied customer per month – 12 additional units on rent
- Add one more rental per month with a superior phone sales presentation – 12 additional units on rent
- Be creative with your unit mix and try to figure out how to rent just one more unit per quarter that you otherwise would not have rented – 4 additional units on rent.

A total of 52 additional units on rent just by being more focused on renting units and understanding the urgency of gaining occupancy.

Step Two: Reduce discounts

A second consideration in the revenue increase exercise is to learn how to reduce discounts whether they are move-in or customer service in nature.

"Giving away FREE rent, for any reason, reduces your rental income"

There are two distinct types of rental discounts, or 'allowances':

- **Rent Allowances:**
  - FREE rent given for customer service issues
  - FREE rent on an account to compensate for a mistake
  - Any other FREE rent applied to an account which reduces the amount of actual rent the tenant must pay.
  - It is important to implement operational procedures that reduce customer service issues.
  - Management should work to eliminate errors that necessitate giving away free rent.

- **Move in Discounts:**
  - Any amount of FREE rent given when a new tenant moves in (1st month free, 50% first month, etc)
  - Referral discounts

Notes to consider when deciding on implementation of move-in discounts:

- Remember that not EVERY customer needs a 'deal' to move in. Managers have to learn to use better judgment about who does and who does not need some incentive to encourage a move in. A person who is clearly shopping around a number of competitors likely will need more of an incentive than a person who pulls in right before closing time in a Uhaul truck full of furniture.
- Learn to use the 'Butt' discount! Unless their 'butt' is walking out the door don't be so quick to give away free rent that you will never get back.

- Investing in training professional sales skills clearly reduces the need for using discounts.
  - Offering features and benefits
  - Using price stalls

If you do find yourself needing to offer move-in discounts that involve free rent:

- Make the discount immediate.
  - Evidence suggests that offering any 'deals' other than for the first month are far less effective. Prospective tenants want to know what they need TODAY to move in. Offering a deal for the 2nd or 3rd month has much less impact. You end up giving away rent that you most likely did not need to.

- Make any move-in discounts short-term.
  - Offering a rent reduction for the first month is almost always incentive enough to encourage a customer to rent (combined with effective sales skills). Offering discounts for 2nd, 3rd and 4th months is giving away rent that almost certainly is not necessary.

- Resist the temptation to discount street rates.
  - It is important to maintain integrity of your street rates. If almost no tenants are paying the posted street rates then you are probably fooling yourself with rates that are too high.

Implementing processes to reduce both of these types of discounts will increase your rental income:

- Make sure that all management clearly understands that issuing any type of rent allowance or discount is giving away free rent.
    - Ask your managers: 'What if was your money? Would you be so quick to give it away?'

Step Three: Increase Street Rental Rates

How to Implement Street Rate Increases

Effective street rate management is one of the most important roles management can play in successfully managing the revenue of a self storage facility.

Although there is no 'perfect system' for managing street rates, there are a couple of fundamental points:

- Increasing street rates is tougher to do with **poorly trained managers.**
    - Poor sales skills have to rely on low rental rates.
    - It is not an accident that in market after market we find that the most professional, highly skilled managers also have the highest rates AND the highest occupancy levels.
- **Not fair** to increase rates on a dirty facility.
- The rates might not 'stick' if your facility has **poor curb appeal**.
- Make sure you have no **out of date signage**.
- Do you have **dated marketing programs**?
- If you are going to charge more you need to **look like you are worth more**!

- **It is important to have a System**; whether it's once a year, once a quarter, once a month or once a week, it is important to create and implement a regular system for review of street rates.
  - Depending on your occupancy and business cycle you may decide to review quarterly in the fall and winter, monthly in the spring, weekly in the summer.
- **Decide on the Pertinent Factors**: What factors should you use when making decisions about whether or not to adjust your street rates?
  - **Check your current occupancy levels**: what do you have to rent?
  - **Know the Competition**: What is everyone else doing?
  - **Calculate your 'Effective' rates**: Are you currently getting your street rates?
- **Decide on your parameters**: What occupancy levels and what ranges, up or down, are you willing to use when deciding on rate adjustments?

'The most important reason for paying MORE attention to rate management is to leave less and less potential revenue on the table'

The MOST important factor you should use when deciding on rate adjustments is your own site's current status and its occupancy:

- If a particular unit size is 90% occupied and you are substantially getting your posted rate, it is time to raise the rate; it should not matter what the market rate is for that unit size.

'You can get higher rates than the market! A great manager using an effective sales presentation far outweighs the pressure to have the lowest prices'

DON'T LET THE COMPETITION DICTATE YOUR PRICES! Competition is A factor, but not THE factor when deciding on adjusting rates.

- **Learn to boost occupancy by increasing rates**

    - Are your 10x10 units highly occupied but not 10x15 units?
        - Increase 10x10 rates to make the 10x15 size more attractive as an option.
    - Learn to increase the rates of sizes larger and smaller than the size you want to 'move'.
    - We do NOT recommend running size specific specials.
        - '10x10 $79!' not very effective, we assume public will recognize what a great deal they'll be getting but without any context they won't know if that's a good deal or not.
        - People rent WHEN they need it and rent the SIZE they need.

Don't make these common mistakes when deciding about adjusting your posted street rates:

- Decide it is too much trouble and just leave the rates in place.
    - Maximizing rental rates on your existing inventory is a critical aspect of increasing revenues and value.
    - We have audited self storage facilities that have used the same street rates for years with no consideration of occupancy levels.
- Have a knee jerk reaction to a competitors change in rates.
    - Just because a competitor lowers or raises a particular rate does not necessarily indicate you should do the same.

- Only take occupancy levels into account without factoring in the EFFECTIVE rate.
  - If you have a size that is 90% physically occupied but only has a 60% economic occupancy percentage then your managers are likely not garnering the current street rates anyway and increasing that rate would not be particularly productive.

Step Four: Increase Rents for Existing Tenants

Raising Rates on Existing Tenants

'Far too many self storage operators NEVER raise tenant rates due to lack of knowledge and fear'

Why Raise Rates?

- EVERYTHING GOES UP! Doesn't your cost of doing business increase year after year? Anyone who rents anything knows that rates go up on a fairly regular basis.

- YOU'RE NOT A 'NOT-FOR-PROFIT' BUSINESS! It's perfectly okay to want to make money in the self storage business and to maximize your efforts to do so.

- YOU HAVE DONE SUCH A GREAT JOB WITH EVERYTHING ELSE THAT YOU HAVE BEEN ABLE TO RAISE YOUR STREET RATES! If you have raised your street rates, why do you still have tenants renting from you for less than the current street rates?

Just as in implementing street rate changes, the most important point to make in a discussion regarding raising rates on existing tenants it to **HAVE A SYSTEM** in place.

- Consider implementing regular increases on tenant anniversary dates.
    - Only exposes 1/12 of your tenant base to an increase at any one time.
    - Do not increase every tenant at the same time.
    - Spreads out the work and the 'pain'.
    - Regular, yearly increases more likely to 'stick' than large increases every 4 or 5 years.
    - Far too much research indicates that moderate increases are worth the effort.
- Increases should be consistent and fair across ALL tenants.
    - No 'special' customers.
    - No 'picking and choosing' who gets increases and who does not.
    - You MIGHT give consideration to tenants with multiple units.
    - Take the 'personality' and manager's favoritism out of the process.
- Implement increases by percentage, not dollar amounts.
    - Not fair to give same $5 increase to tenant with a 5x5 and tenant with a 10x30.
- Send increases out with at least a 30 day notice.
- Tenants on auto-billing are much less likely to move due to an increase...make your 'No Late Fee Guarantee' program a BIG deal!
- Important to maintain a superior customer service atmosphere at your facility
    - Clean
    - Maintenance items taken care of in a timely manner
    - Friendly & welcoming staff
    - Under promise and over deliver
    - Exceed expectations

- Tenants are more resistant to pay more for an inferior product.
- Implement a policy that tenants more than 30 days past due AUTOMATICALLY receive a rent increase to at least the current street rate.
  - Not unusual to get a penalty for paying late.
  - Why should past due customers get any consideration related to a reduced rate?
  - If unit is liquidated at auction any past rental rate increases will reduce the amount the tenant might receive from their liquidated unit.

How can you successfully implement tenant rate increases?

- **Accept the fact** that some tenants may move out. You can't afford to be 'held hostage' by your fear that some tenants may leave.
- **Commit to a systematic process;** once a year on the tenant's anniversary date is a common and effective process.
- **Decide on an amount and stick to it;** depending on your outlook for the year and what you have been able to do with your posted street rates, make a decision about how much of a raise you are going to implement; is it 3% this year? Or 5%?
- **Make sure everyone's on board;** rent raise are much more successful if EVERYONE from the site manager to the owner agrees on the process and understands why it is necessary
- **Be willing to think outside the box;** depending on circumstances, you may have to implement increases more often than planned and for more than you first thought; self storage is a 'supply and demand' business; if you have been able to raise your rates higher than previously thought due to market conditions and your own success, be willing to increase existing tenants more aggressively than first planned.

DO NOT BE AFRAID TO IMPLEMENT EXISTING TENANT RATE INCREASES!

Step Five: Increase Ancillary Income

Increasing Fee Income

Although not as substantial an amount as rental income, the degree to which you work to increase your fee income will have a positive impact on your bottom line.

There are four primary fees that the typical self storage facility charges:

- **Administration fees**: normally charged on each new rental; this fee pays for the processing of new paperwork, the customers files, etc. Also called 'set-up' or 'new account' fees
- **Delinquent fees**: these are fees charged by the existing late fees schedule in place at your site; more and more these fees are dictated by state law, so make sure you are in compliance.
  - Make sure your late fees are clearly outlined in the lease agreement.
- **Lien Fees**: most self storage sites assess a fee for beginning the lien process; this fee covers the costs of following the state lien laws, including preparing the unit for auction, certified mail and legal advertising.
- **NSF fees**: legal fee charged on an account for issuing a bad check.

Steps to Increasing Fee Income

1. Don't apologize for any fees. Expect all new tenants to pay the administration fee, all past due customers to pay late fees and all lien customers to pay the lien fees.
2. Don't waive late fees; as long as you have clearly stated your late fee policy in your lease agreement, there is no reason to waive a late fee.
   a. Have a consistent and firm policy
   b. Never play favorites
   c. Never apologize
   d. Keep in mind that you are not 'adding late fees'; your late tenants are 'earning' late fees by choosing to pay late
3. Clearly explain your lease and have the tenant initial next to those fees.
4. Once you initiate the lien process, NEVER waive your lien fees

Remember that there is no point in having a late fee policy if you aren't going to stick to it. You will find that tenants are LESS upset about having to pay late fees if you refuse to waive the first one than if you waive the first one but refuse to waive the next one; once you waive the first one, you will be expected to waive all of them

Increasing Ancillary Income

Another important revenue source for most self storage facilities is Ancillary Income: merchandise sales, truck rental revenue and insurance collections.

Points to help increase your merchandise sales:

- Mention with EVERY customer contact:
  - new customers
  - existing customers
  - vacating customers
  - prospects
  - All receipts and tenant correspondence should mention your ancillary products and services.

Never ask a customer 'do you need any boxes?" but instead ask "have you started packing your things yet?

Asking a 'yes or no' question will usually get a NO; asking a 'probing' question starts a conversation. If the customer says 'we're going to get some boxes from behind the liquor store' then you have a chance to sell against that, sell them on the benefits of using your boxes instead.

- Keep your merchandise well stocked, clean and fresh.
  - An anemic or confusing display indicates that you are not really interested in selling merchandise.
- Merchandise needs to be clearly priced.
  - If you have to keep checking the computer for prices the customer will become annoyed.
- Know your products features and benefits.
  - You should know, for example, that books should be stored in small boxes and pillows in large boxes.

- Expect to sell merchandise.
  - Assume the sale! Use phrases like 'most of our customers usually find that a bundle of small boxes works best; do you feel a bundle will be enough for your needs?'
- Add-on sales; never sell a box without suggesting tape or bubble wrap.
- Suggestive selling; if someone wants to buy boxes, find out why...they may need peanuts, bubble wrap or wrapping paper.
- ALWAYS BE SELLING!
  - From the first contact with the prospective tenant to the closing of the sale to every time they make their payment you should be mentioning the availability of your merchandise.
- Assume lock sales; you should always take at least two choices of lock whenever you show a prospective tenant their space.
- After taking your customer on a property tour to look at storage units we highly recommend that you then walk over to your merchandise display and continue the sales process there. You will sell more merchandise standing next to the merchandise than you will from behind the counter.

'Realize that when you fail to sell your customers the extra packing supplies and moving materials they need to complete their storage experience...someone else will'

Points to help increase your truck rental revenues

One of the most effective marketing tools that self storage sites have added in the past several years is the availability of truck rentals at their facility.

A LARGE percentage of self storage customers do use moving trucks to move in and out of their space, so it only makes sense to add that availability when possible; adding a truck can truly make your site a 'one stop shop' for all the needs of your customers.

If you do have or intend to add truck rentals to your site:

- NEVER ask "Do you need a truck" but instead ask "Have you decided how to move your goods into storage?" Remember; NEVER ask a Yes or No question in sales.
  - If a potential customer says 'I'm borrowing my brother's pickup truck' then you have the opportunity to sell them on the benefits of instead renting your truck.
- Mention truck rentals to every potential customer
- Realize that ALL customers are potential truck customers; new move ins, vacating tenants and your existing customers.
- Keep your truck clean and well maintained.
- Know your competitor's rates and policies.

Points to help increase your insurance collections

A significant number of self storage sites now offer some type of tenant goods insurance coverage to their customers for their stored goods. Should you be one of those sites, use the following to help increase your insurance collections:

- Realize that you are providing your customers a great deal of customer service by offering peace of mind for the protection of their goods.
- Always offer two positive options; 'Would $2000 in coverage meet your needs or would $5000 be more appropriate?" NEVER ask 'do you need insurance?"
- By offering an affordable insurance coverage, you are also creating peace of mind for the site managers because if anything ever does happen that requires insurance it makes the manager's job easier if the tenant can call the insurance company.
- Most policies amount to only pennies per day

Step Six: Improve Collections

"Once you figure out how to rent more units, you then have to figure out how to effectively collect the rent"

Self storage is, at its core, a fundamentally simple premise: you rent space and then collect the rent. Unfortunately, many self storage operators fail to do a good job of the collections half of this simple formula.

There are three simple yet critical steps to increasing collections and maximizing the amount of rent you can collect on your existing tenant base:

- Effectively manage your accounts receivable.
  - Clearly explain the rental lease upon unit rental; do not 'shy away' from reviewing the late fees and the lien process.
  - Work your tenant late list with a regular and systematic plan.
  - Follow through on the late fee schedule and lien process as allowed by your state laws.
  - Make time for working on late tenant lists early in the process because you will spend more time later if you don't.
- Expect your customers to pay their full balance
  - You should not manage your self storage site as a 'non-profit organization'; your tenant signed a lease agreement and agreed to pay a particular monthly rent payment and agreed to pay the rent on time.
  - Collect all rent AND fees due.
  - If a tenant comes in to pay near the end of their current rental period, expect them to pay the next period's payment as well.
- Utilize whatever account management procedures afforded you by law.
  - Lock tenants out of their units as soon as the law allows.
  - Do not hesitate to follow through on lien and auction procedures.

Remember: as long as you are providing the product and services you agreed to perform as part of the self storage relationship, you must expect the customer to do the same.

- Utilize an Effective Training program
  - Do your managers know how to maximize their collection efforts to increase revenues?
- Expect a clear Understanding of potential rent values
  - Does everyone know how much they can collect?
  - If not you are traveling without a map!

- Prepare clearly defined guidelines and expectations
  - What are your goals?
  - How do you know if you did a good job?
- Instruct managers to quit waiving late fees
  - Tenants earn late fees, we don't assess them
  - Managers need to 'own' the policy and quit blaming it on the company.
  - Resist the tendency to chose favorites and take path of least resistance.
- Take steps to reduce auctions
  - The best auction is no auction
  - We lose money on auctions most of the time
  - Make sure good information is gathered when person first becomes a tenant

Reduce your non-standard rentals

'As long as your rates are competitive and you have a strong rental sales presentation, you should expect tenants to pay your posted rates"

Many self storage sites don't have an 'occupancy' issue as much as they have an 'occupant' issue; there are too many occupants NOT paying the correct street rates.

There are various reasons this happens:

- Street rates have increased
- Competitor rates have been matched
- Specials have been implemented
- Too much 'price matching' and not enough effective sales presentation

How can you reduce the non-standard rents and increase rental income?

- **Implement an effective sales presentation!** An effective sales presentation reduces the downward pressure on rates.
- **Know your competitor rates**
  - Keeps you competitive
  - You can match rates, when necessary, with pertinent information
- **Have an effective 'rent-raise' process in place**
- **Be aware** of unit mix, occupancy levels and opportunities for rent increases
- **Utilize any move-in promotions correctly**; if the site has a '3 months at 25% off' move-in promotion, make sure the rate increases to the correct rate after 3 months.

Reduce Uncollected Rent

'You can increase your rental income by reducing the amount of time a tenant is allowed to use your space for free'

'Uncollected rent' is any amount of rent that is owed but never collected; although it is almost impossible to eliminate uncollected rent, there are certainly points to be made in mitigating those losses:

- **EFFECTIVELY** manage the past due tenant list
  - Implement an effective plan to work the list and stick to it
  - Expect tenants to pay
  - Consider tenants past due when they are 1 day delinquent; the longer you wait to contact tenants about their past due balance, the more they will owe and the more likely it is they will attempt to move out without paying rent

- Understand and implement your lien process in a timely manner
    - AS SOON as allowed by law, start the lien process. The more you stall, the more likely it is that you will end up selling a unit for far less than is owed and in the meantime, you are tying up a unit that should be collecting rent
    - Be willing to 'make deals' with tenants in lien; you are far more likely to receive more rent from a past due tenant than from a bidder at auction.
- Realize that the collection process starts with getting a good rental application with as much contact information as possible and clearly explaining the lease.
- Restrict unit access as quickly as allowed by law.
- Be aware of what's going on at your site; many tenants skip out owing rent in plain sight of management.

MOST tenants do not enter into a self storage relationship with your site with the intention of moving their goods into storage and never returning or paying rent. Don't take their lateness or apparent disinterest in paying for their goods personally.

Understanding Basic Reporting to Effectively Manage Your Revenue

Although software programs vary widely and there are several quality choices, they all have several basic management reports in common.

It is important that you understand these reports and the information they relay in an effort to better understand the revenue management of your site.

All programs have a 'Summary' report that provides a 'snap-shot' of a given period and helps management understand the revenue situation of a site:

- Occupancy: whether measured by number of units or amount of square footage, this number indicates how much of the facility is rented.
- Gross Potential Rent: this is the $ amount of rent your site COULD collected if the site were 100% occupied at the posted street rates.
- Actual Rent: this is the $ of rent your site COULD collect on the current tenant base at their current rates.
- Financial occupancy: this percentage number is a function of the total amount of actual rent that COULD be collected if all tenants were paying the posted street rates the site were full and the amount of rent that CAN be collected on the current tenant base.
  - For example, if your site had a POTENTIAL rent of $50,000 and an ACTUAL rent of $30,000, the FINANCIAL OCCUPANCY of the site would be 60%

- Ideally, your Physical OCCUPANCY % and your FINANCIAL OCCUPANCY % should be the same;
  - The SPREAD between these two numbers can be accounted for in a couple of or in a combination of ways:
    - Non-standard rents
    - Street rate increase and decreases
  - The larger the difference between the physical occupancy and the financial occupancy, the more tenants you have paying less or more than the current street rates.
- Accounts receivable: this will be the number of accounts and the amount of money that remains uncollected but due.
- Move in discounts: this is the $ amount of FREE rent given at the time of new move-ins. This number should reflect the current move in promotion
- Rent allowances: this is the amount of FREE rent given for various reasons; customer service issues, errors, etc.
- Late fees waived: amount of fees that have been waived from accounts
- Vacate uncollected (bad debt, skips, etc); this is the amount of rent that was due but now has gone uncollected due to a skip or a unit having been sold at auction.

'No matter the process or program, it is critical to have systems in place to monitor these crucial revenue management numbers'

The revenue management formula is a simple one:

1. **increase rental income**: rent more units, rent them for the correct rates, reduce non standard rents
2. **reduce move in discounts**: develop a professional sales presentation, manage effectively and as determined by the market
3. **reduce rent allowances:** superior customer service, fewer mistakes
4. **reduce uncollected rent:** have fewer auctions, clearly explain lease, be aware of what's going on at site
5. **increase fee income:** don't waive fees, collect what is due
6. **increase ancillary revenues:** improved merchandise, truck and insurance revenues

All of this adds up to increased revenues and a more effective revenue management system!

Why Should You Bother Implementing a Revenue Management System:

There are Residual Benefits of the Revenue Increase Exercise:
- **Sustained Discipline**
- **Accountability**
- **Continued Appreciation**
- **Market Positioning**

Sustained Discipline

- Implementing revenue management techniques puts operational systems in place that are more likely to handle the challenges in the markets.
- What if you decided to sell? Having such systems in place will keep your self storage asset 'sell-ready' at all times in order to maximize potential values.

Accountability

- Clearly communicating the revenues management systems in place will allow onsite management to more clearly understand the goals and requirements of ownership.

Continued Appreciation

- Value increase systems go on autopilot and are less subject to personalities and uninformed opinions.

Market Positioning

- You can develop a more clear understanding of your facility's place in the market if you have automated systems in place that manage rates and maximize all channels of revenue and value enhancement.

The Bottom Line to Implementing Effective Revenue and Value Increase Policies and Procedures:

- Implementing revenue management plans at your facility will increase the value of your storage assets.

- The efforts to increase revenues are worthy of your time and energy to implement.

- EVERY dollar increase will add to the value of your self storage assets.

- Professional self storage operators find opportunities to increase revenues even in the most challenging of economic climates.

About the Author

Bob Copper has worked extensively in the self storage industry for many years, amassing vast experience in effective operational systems, successful marketing initiatives and asset value creation. He has traveled around the country conducting countless due diligence projects, operational audits, market studies and training assignments within the self-storage industry. Bob is known throughout the self storage industry for his no-nonsense approach to improving operations, profits and values and is sought out for his unbiased and professional opinion in all self storage related discussions.

His consulting firm, Self Storage 101, with offices in Alabama and California, is among the largest in the industry and is recognized as one of the few firms capable of large projects and assignments. His team of professionals has vast experience in development, management, turn-around, and vendor contacts and has a unique understanding of all aspects of the self-storage industry. They also provide industry leading training programs, extensive workshops, up to date manuals and other industry-specific materials.

Bob has a Bachelor's Degree from Stetson University in Deland, FL. He speaks frequently at industry gatherings and has written extensively for industry publications.

Bob can be reached at 866-269-1311 and you can find out more about Self Storage 101 at www.selfstorage101.com.

Made in the USA
Columbia, SC
30 August 2023

22250829R00022